LITTLE JOHNNY'S CONFESSION

By Brian Patten

Notes to the Hurrying Man
The Elephant and the Flower
The Irrelevant Song
Jumping Mouse

LITTLE JOHNNY'S CONFESSION

by Brian Patten

London
George Allen and Unwin Ltd

First published in 1967
Second Impression 1967
Third Impression 1969
Fourth Impression 1970
Fifth Impression 1971
Sixth Impression 1973

ISBN 0 04 821013 7 Cased
       0 04 821014 5 Paper

Printed in Great Britain
in 10pt. Univers type
by Compton Printing Ltd
London and Aylesbury

For Maureen
with love

Acknowledgements are made to the following
in which some of these poems have appeared :
*Transatlantic Review, The Listener, Poetry
Review* (The Poetry Society), *Solstice* (Cambridge),
Peace News, New Poems (1965) (P.E.N.),
Evergreen Review, The Scotsman, and the BBC
Third Programme.

CONTENTS

LITTLE JOHNNY'S CONFESSION

This morning
  being rather young and foolish
  I borrowed a machinegun my father
  had left hidden since the war, went out,
  and eliminated a number of small enemies.
  Since then I have not returned home.

This morning
  swarms of police with trackerdogs
  wander about the city
  with my description printed
  on their minds, asking:
  'Have you seen him?
  He is seven years old,
  likes Pluto, Mighty Mouse
  and Biffo the Bear,
  have you seen him, anywhere?'

This morning
  sitting alone in a strange playground
  muttering you've blundered, you've blundered
  over and over to myself
  I work out my next move
  but cannot move.
  The trackerdogs will sniff me out,
  they have my lollypops.

LITTLE JOHNNY'S FOOLISH INVENTION
A Fable for Atomic Adam

One day
> while playing with old junk in the attic
> Little Johnny accidentally invented an atomic bomb
> and not knowing what to do with it
> buried it in the front garden.

Next morning
> during cornflakes and sunrise
> he noticed it glowing damp among the cabbages
> and so took it out
> out into the city
> where it smelt of tulips
> but was sadly inedible.

What can I do with it, he sighed, having nowhere to hide it?
I'm afraid that soon a busy policeman might come along
to detain me. I'd make a statement. Say

> I'd like a new bomb, a blue bomb,
a bomb I could explode in dormitories
where my friends are sleeping,
that would not wake them or shake them but
would simply keep them from weeping;
> a bomb I could bounce in the playground
and spray over flowers, a bomb
that would light the Universe for years and send down
showers of joy.

> But he'd pay no attention he
> would simply take out his notebook and write:
> This child is mad.
> This child is a bomb.

★ ★ ★

Last night in my nightmares
    the bomb became transparent
    and through it my atomic friends wandered, naked
    but for a few carefully placed leaves
    that were continually rotting.

So now looking much older
    I trace about obscure cities
    looking for a place to leave my bomb
    but am always turned away by minor officials
    who say, 'It's a deterrent,' and I answer, 'Sure!'

It will deter
    flowers and birds and the sunlight from calling
    and one morning
    at sunrise when I rise and glow
    I'll look outside to make certain my invention has not
                                    bloomed
    but will see nothing through
    the melting windows.

This afternoon
    while looking for hidden meanings in Superman
    And discussing tadpole collections
    I discovered I belonged to Generation X
    And developed numerous complexes;
    I turned on to Gothic fairytales and Alister Crowley,
    Equated Batman with homosexuality, so

Please Mr. Teacher, Sir,
Turn round from your blackboard,
The whole class has its hands up,
We're in rather a hurry.
The desks are returning to forests,
The inkwells overflowing,
The boys in the backrow have drowned.
Please Mr. Teacher, Sir,
Turn round from your blackboard,
Your chalks are crumbling,
Your cane's decaying,
Turn round from your blackboard
We're thinking of leaving.

This afternoon
    a quiet criminal moves through the classroom
    Deciding on his future;
    Around him, things have fallen apart—
    Something's placed an inkstained finger
    On his heart.

LITTLE JOHNNY TAKES A TRIP TO ANOTHER PLANET

Through his bedroom window, later they confirmed
Johnny drifted one Monday evening
Up above the sleeping world.

He left this message :

I've taken a trip to another planet
And I'll be away for a while,
so don't send the Escaped Children Squad after me
the Universe is too wild.

Now among black glass trees
he weaves intricate shapes
in a world an inch away from ours,
and from behind his eyes
he sees into a waiting room of light
and maps out the route dawn takes through
the nurseries of night.

He has switched on a world and walked inside ;
and as silence blooms among the flowers
he wonders at people groping
through transparent hours.
He's found the perfect loophole :
sits on the other side,
a child with eyes as big as planets
whose dreams do not collide
with any forms of teaching
with any form of lies.

So don't send the Escaped Children Squad after him
he'll be away for a while,
he's taken a trip to another planet
and the Universe is too wild
for him to make it back
in the same state of mind.

LITTLE JOHNNY'S FINAL LETTER

Mother,
       I won't be home this evening, so
       don't worry; don't hurry to report me missing.
       Don't drain the canals to find me,
       I've decided to stay alive, don't
       search the woods, I'm not hiding,
       simply gone to get myself classified.
       Don't leave my shreddies out,
       I've done with security.
       Don't circulate my photograph to society
       I have disguised myself as a man
       and am giving priority to obscurity.
       It suits me fine;
       I have taken off my short trousers
       and put on long ones, and
       now am going out into the city, so
       don't worry; don't hurry to report me missing.

       I've rented a room without any curtains
       and sit behind the windows growing cold,
       heard your plea on the radio this morning,
       you sounded sad and strangely old. . . .

AH JOHNNY WHAT WHEN YOU'RE OLDER?

Ah Johnny,
What when you are older?
The Humphrey Bogart of Innocence
Wandering gangster fashion through your dreams?
What fantasies will you have
When finding Alice in some sunny glade
She lies down and says
'OK, Let's make it'.

Johnny will you still be sane when Winnie the Pooh
Grows into some gigantic bear
And comes to mawl you?
When Archie attacks Mehitabel,
When Mr. Toad finally crashes and Toad Hall perishes
With only the willows as witnesses?

When Brer Rabbit commits harikari in a decaying tree-trunk
Will you report the incident
Or simply shrug your shoulders and wander away?

You'll find no magic potions, no strange herbs,
No bodies blushing with light—You'll grow podgy!
Buttoned up to the neck with respectability!
Already you're wearing pink shirts! Bright shining shoes!
Johnny this is my last poem about you,
I'm afraid to remember what you were.
You'll find nothing when you've grown,
When all your routines are established,
When the last young thigh you'll ever encounter
Turns round and machineguns you down.

Soon you will climb into a bus full of schoolchildren
And asking for a single back to innocence
Will collapse among the used tickets
Groaning some illegible ode nobody will remember.

PROSE POEM TOWARDS A DEFINITION OF ITSELF

When in public poetry should take off its clothes and wave to the nearest person in sight; It should be seen in the company of thieves and lovers rather than that of journalists and publishers. On sighting mathematicians it should unhook the algebra from their minds and replace it with poetry; on sighting poets it should unhook poetry from the minds and replace it with algebra: it should touch those people who despise being touched, it should fall in love with children and woo them with fairytales; it should wait on the landing for two years for its mates to come home then go outside and find them all dead.

When the electricity fails it should wear dark glasses and pretend to be blind. It should guide those who are safe into the middle of busy roads and leave them there. It should scatter woodworm into the bedrooms of all peglegged men, not being afraid to hurt the innocent; It should shout EVIL! EVIL! EVIL! from the roofs of stock exchanges. It should not pretend to be a clerk or a librarian. It is the eventual sameness of contradictions. It should never weep unless it is alone, and then only after it has covered the mirrors and sealed up the cracks.

Poetry should seek out pale and lyrical couples and wander with them into stables, neglected bedrooms, engineless cars, unsafe forests, for A Final Good Time. It should enter burning factories too late to save anybody. It should pay no attention to its name.

Poetry should be seen lying by the side of road accidents, hissing from unlit gas-rings. It should scrawl the nymphs secret on her teachers blackboard, offer her a worm saying: Inside this is a tiny apple. At dawn it should leave the bedroom and catch the first bus home to its wife. At dusk it should chat up a girl nobody wants. It should be seen standing on the ledge of a skyscraper, on a bridge with a brick tied around its heart. Poetry is the monster hiding in a child's dark room, it is the scar on a beautiful person's face. It is the last blade of grass being picked from the city park.

A THEME FOR VARIOUS MURDERS

She walks alone by the river
   her adolescent breasts
     and eyes
      and hips
       and legs as well
that were once so cool around her schoolboy lover
  now move in time to dreams of her body's gangster
   waiting naked for her
     in a place where it is silent
       except for the downpour.

Lately she has become aware
  of her own movements;
    next to her body
    she wears very little;
She has heard of the freedom that like rain
  runs loose about the city
      —and being no different than her age,
      being only her age,
      she lies open to new possibilities
and quick, new birds twitter in her blood.

But
  the gangster
    will dullen her,
      and he who will disappear eventually
shall machinegun down her innocence
  and we will find her only
    when all that's precious
      is dead in her.

Where is
  the schoolboy lover,
    tell me
      where is he?

Not down by that river
   but minute among his fantasies
      with potent secretaries
         who rise at dawn from his mind,
            damp and warm,
               and come out of his eyes

   while she walks there
      alone this evening,
   while she walks
      with the last crazy song
   about to die in her.

WHERE ARE YOU NOW SUPERMAN?

The serials are all wound up now,
Put away in small black boxes
For a decade or so. Superman's asleep
In the sixpenny childhood seats,
Batman and Robin are elsewhere
And can't see the Batsign thrown out
By kids with toffee-smeared mouths.
Captain Marvel's SHAZAM! echoes round the auditorium,
But the magicians don't hear him,
Must all be dead. . . .
The Purple Monster who came down from the Purple Planet
Disguised as a man, is wandering aimlessly about the streets
With no way of getting back.
Sir Galahad's been strangled by the Incredible Living Trees,
Zorro killed by his own sword.
Blackhawk's buried his companions
In the disused hangers of innocence
And Flash Gordon likewise wanders lonely,
Weeping over the girl he loved 7 Universes ago.

We killed them all simply because we grew up;
We made them possible with our uneducated minds
And with our pocket money
And the sixpences we received
For pretending to be Good.
We think we are too old to cheer and boo now,
But let's not kid ourselves,
We still cheer and boo
But do it quietly or at General Elections
Where its still possible to find a goodie
Now and then.

Clark Kent (alias Superman)
Committed suicide because he failed to find new roles.
The bullets that bounced off him on the screen
Wormed their way in in Real Life.
But who cared for real life?
We had our own world, our own celluloid imaginations
And now we have a different world,
One that's a little more cynical
And we believe, a little more real.

Our batsignals now questions flung into space
To attract the attention of passing solutions. . . .

A CREATURE TO TELL THE TIME BY

I created for myself
a creature to tell the time by
    —& on the lawns of her tongue
flowers grew,
    sweet scented words fell
out her mouth, her eyes and paws were
                  comforting—
    & woken with her
    at dawn, with living birds

humming, alien
inside my head,

I noticed inside us both
the green love that grew there yesterday
was dead.

THE ASTRONAUT

We will take a trip
to the planets inside us,
where love is the astronaut

alone at last, not caring
what planet he lands on, and he,
free to glide between

what is said and
what is understood
by saying it,

sees how the Universe decays
while men find ways
of mending it.

SING SOFTLY

Sing softly
now sadly
of rains he has known,

of dawns when
his visions
were of dampboys

slim and brown,
walking at the edge
of cold rivers.

O they were once
the palest of children,
stripping.

Slim fish
darting through water
laughing now and then.

SEASCAPE

gulls kiss the sun
and you walk on the beach
afraid of the tide

from the sea's warm belly
a lobster crawls to
see if we've gone

but mouths still talk
and finding out my lips
I say to you ;

'lay silently,
stretch out your arms
like seaweed strangled by the wind.'

you answer with silence
as tears drip from
the roof of your womb

out of a seashell
a sandcrab pokes his head
and sniffs the salt wind

now afraid we sit in silence
and watching the sun go down
I ask you your name

SCHOOLBOY

Before playtime let us consider the possibilities
of getting stoned on milk.

In his dreams,
scribling overcharged on woodbines,
mumbling obscure sentences into his desk
'No way of getting out,
no way out. . . .'

          Poet dying of
too much education, schoolgirls, examinations,
canes that walk the nurseries of his wet dreams;
satchels full of chewing gum; bad jokes, pencils;
crude drawings performed in the name of art. Soon will
come the Joyful Realisation in Mary's back kitchen
      while mother's out.
All this during chemistry.

(The headmaster's crying in his study.
His old pinstriped pants rolled up to his knees
in a vain attempt to recapture youth; emotions
skid along his slippery age; Love, smeared across his face,
like a road accident.)

The schoolyard's full of people to hate.
Full of tick and prefects and a fat schoolmaster
and whistles and older and younger boys, but
he's growing,
    sadly
       growing
         up.

Girls,
    becoming mysterious, are now more important
than arriving at school late or receiving trivial awards.
Postcards of those huge women
                seem a little more believable now.
(Secretly, the pale, unmarried headmaster telling him
Death is the only grammatically correct full-stop.)
Girls,
    still mysterious;
arithmetic thighed, breasts measured in thumb prints,
not inches.
Literature's just another way out.
History's full of absurd mistakes.
King Arthur hardly ever existed
and if he had he'd have only have farted and
excused himself from the Round Table in a hurry.

(The headmaster, staring through the study window
into the playground, composes evil poems about
the lyrical boy in class four.)
                'He invited us up sir,
            but not for the cane,
                said the algebra of life
                    was far too difficult to explain
                    and that all equations
                        mounted to nothing . . .'
Growing up's wonderful if
    you keep
        your eyes
            closed tightly,
and if you grow up
    take your soul with you,
        nobody wants it.

So,
playtime's finished with;
it's time to pull the last sad chain
                on his last
                    sadschoolgirlcrush.

27

It is time to fathom out too many things.
To learn he's no longer got somebody watching over him;
he's going to know strange things, learn
how to lie correctly, how to lay correctly,
how to cheat and steal in the nicest possible manner.
He will learn among other things, how to enjoy
his enemies and how to avoid friendships. If he's unlucky
he will learn how to love and give everything away
and how eventually, he'll end up with nothing.

    He won't understand many things.
He'll just accept them. He'll experiment with hardboiled
                eggs all his life
and die a stranger in a race attempting humanity.

    And finally,
the playground full of dust,
    crates of sour milk lining the corridors:
        the headmaster, weeping quietly among the saws
                          and chisels
      in the damp woodwork room.

      The ghosts of Tim and Maureen and Pat
     and Nancy and so many others,
   all holding sexless hands, all doomed to living, and
one pale boy
in a steamy room
looking outside across the roofs and chimneys
where it seems, the clouds are crying,
the daylight's gone blind
and his teachers, all dead.

DELICATE JOHN

Delicate John has moved away.
Listen to what the children said :

He couldn't make love
And he couldn't make money,
He had a gammy leg
(which they thought was funny).

Now John, tender and quiet as a habit,
Is leading half a life among his books.
He cannot return from where he came
Because the children learnt

Of what they thought a lack of love,
Of his lack of money,
Of something unfamiliar in his brain
(which they thought was funny)

He sits at a window and sometimes they pass,
Those who gave him a monkey for his back,
They pass in twos they pass in threes,
They look contented, they look pleased
And John sits and he rots away
Behind a lace curtain where he quietly cries
Tears as big as a choir boy's eyes.

What have they done to John,
What have they done to him?
The children who grow old,
Who squabble and grow thin,
Who lick their lips at disaster
And quietly whisper of sin.

CHEQUE FOR A DREAM

Through the tatter bag rag shouldered years
With a cheque for a dream
But no bank to cash it in
Limps an old woman with a well-worn soul.

Lizzy, you're old now.
Lizzy—the name's laughable.
I remember when I was half your size
Skipping through the pale afternoons,
Bullying my way to the front of the
Saturday Afternoon Matinées,
Carving my initials in a desk where I kept
Illegible writing books.

Funny how I remember, How
Only one of us has changed. How
Like strangers we have become.

Now when I visit you you take me into a corner and,
As ifit were twelve years ago, say : 'Here's
Something for you,' and fumbling in your purse
Find sixpence or perhaps a shilling.
How should I react?
Say thanks and pocket it, or hand it back and say
'I don't need it anymore.'

Through the tatter bag rag shouldered years
With a cheque for a dream
But no bank to cash it in
Limps an old woman with a well-worn soul.

Growing's a strange thing Lizzy,
And I have learnt to forget so much.
I dont think of you very often
But when I do I imagine in a cinema a movie screen
Depicting the tenements and old prams and scenery I
    know so well,

And through it all your sad figure creeps
With Chaplin movements, and sometimes you turn around
And smiling wave at the empty auditorium. But only memories
Clap back and cheer you from the dusty seats.

LAMENT FOR THE ANGELS WHO'VE LEFT MY STREET

There are no angels in my street
Only poems and drawings scrawled in chalk
On the pavements and walls.
The girls have grown up and out and moved away,
Leaving only cheap scent bottles on the sideboard
And Marks and Spencer bras lining the dusty cupboards.
They've gone to seek their misfortunes,
To be made with growing up ideas and suggestions
And with their hot, little-no-longer bodies
Which have become fine since the time
They were touched for the price of a lollypop.

The angels are fading—
And my only consolation is in remembering
I'm living elsewhere now.
Can't say I'd like to be back there,
Among those streets that no longer house any dreams.
Streets everywhere! All peopled by memories and the times
I was a monster and scared my playmates
On backyard walls cutting clotheslines
Keeping impossible monkies in impossible jamjars,
Playing games in the kickthecan streets and swinging
On lamps that were then gas and black.

Angels have gone now—couldn't have bedded them anyway.
First neurotic kiss on a wet step under a tree growing
In a friend's backgarden—Small spies in the darkness
We watched backbedroom windows dreaming nasty
                                         things:
Standing outside cinemas without much hope of getting in,
Chatting up twelve year old girls, without much hope of
                                         getting in;
Swimming in the parks on Sunday afternoons, our clothesspread
Like extra bodies in the green glowing grass.

Angels I was afraid of with my pale fears—
My brain with its secret 'X' certificate
Always was outside the group in my street,
Couldn't skip good, run good, jump good and always
In before the rest of them,
Throwing comics out of the bedroom windows
Just as I throw poems out of my eyes now.

In my street people were mostly happy because they didn't
                    know too much about the state of things,
They didn't want to know too much about the state of things,
And perhaps I should have stayed among them—
But something went wrong.
It was something about the angels that made me go wrong,
Sort of knocked me off course,
Led me away from the factories and cafes,
From the corners of streets where policemen were never kind
And where the ponytailed bobby-socked girls knew all
                            about it.
Then my soul was in an army of paper boats, sailing down
Numerous streets but getting stuck and watching
            The rest float on :
All this because of the angels and their gray attitudes
And their little to be touched only when mum's out breasts.

II.

And now behind a door nobody's bothering to open
I consider my angel—Has she grown stale ?—
Has she faded among newly created misfortunes,
How well does she wear her flesh ?
Street-angel, angel in your street, come to me,
Help me to record things of importance,
To record the sounds our lives make in bumping together,
I want an angel to help me record these things !
And they'll be far from overpoetic statements
And they'll be true,
And I will be left alone in my room in my street
Until death comes and turns me off.

SONG FOR LAST YEAR'S WIFE

Alice, this is my first winter
of waking without you, of knowing
that you, dressed in familiar clothes
are elsewhere, perhaps not even
conscious of our anniversary. Have
you noticed? The earth's still as hard,
the same empty gardens exist? It is
as if nothing special had changed.
I wake with another mouth feeding
from me, but still feel as if
love had not the right
to walk out of me. A year now. So
what? you say. I send out my spies
to find who you are living with, what
you are doing. They return, smile
and tell me your body's as firm,
you are as alive, as warm and inviting
as when they knew you first.
                    Perhaps it is the winter,
its isolation from other seasons, that
sends me your ghost to witness
when I wake. Somebody came here today, asked
how you were keeping, what you were doing.
I imagine you, waking in another city,
touched by this same hour. So
ordinary a thing as loss comes now
and touches me.

ROOM

Room you're toneless now.
Room you don't belong to me
I want another room I want one
without your tatty memories
I want to brush you out into the streets where
you'll become a debris full of childrens laughter
Room you're murderous
You're a crooked woman with armpits full of lice
You're nogood to me
You make me feel like an accident
Make me blush with your crude jokes
and your old iron bedsteads
Room you've made me weep too many times
I'm sick of you and all your faces
I go into houses and find its still you only this time
you're wearing a different disguise
I send out my spies to find you
but they don't return
I send myself out and find you eating my spies.
Its impossible. You stand there dusty and naked
Your records spinning mutely
Your bed throwing gleeming girlbodies at the armies
of wage clerks who prance in you
Your books all empty
Your gasstoves hissing
Wallpaper crying sighing it doesn't matter
for your windows have become tape-recordings of the night
and only death will shove you to sleep.
I'm going to leave you
Going to spend all my dreams
Once in you I could lie and hear the spying moon apologise
as it tiptoed through the clouds
and left you in your special darkness
But it's different now, now

only the rain splatters through
and the only other sound is you whispering
I'm not around you I'm in you all my walls are in you
Room you're full of my own graves!

ON A HORSE CALLED AUTUMN

On a horse called autumn
among certain decaying things
she rides inside me, for

no matter where I move
this puzzled woman sings
of nude horsemen breached
in leather,

of stables decaying near
where once
riders came,

and where now alone
her heart journeys, among
lies I made real.

Now riding in truth
what alterations can I make
knowing nothing will change?

Things stay the same:
Such journeys as her's
are the ones I care for.

THE LAKE

It's a new world.
He wakes beneath a lake
and sits listening to the rain,
the frightful tapping of water on water.
(And the rain asks to be let in
But the lake refuses.)
So he listens in silence,
sometimes stretching out his arms
to feel the rain above him,
but he cannot reach the surface
nor touch the light
and the rain falls.
'Am I so dead that
I cannot touch the rain?'
And there is only silence
as the earth grows darker
and the children hurry home
across damp fields
whispering secrets that echo back
and frighten him.

TO MY OTHER POET

You are standing on the debris
pressed against the sun,
and the firm white birds
and the grass becoming yellow
does not belong to you.
Go under the soil
into obscure fantasies of another damp universe;
though this earth will choke you
it will be yours.

Let no others come
smelling of the rain
and splintered by light:
listen to them!
stomping and screaming obscenities,
vampires of the daylight
wanting to destroy you
and suck from you this blood
obsessed with darkness.

You age,
the tail end of innocence
is drowned in tears,
and you, who know nothing of what is
will kiss earth and star
and break level-headed sanity
and the gleaming eyes of love
will turn blind and rot away.

If ever you exist
(I say if ever you exist)
above a broken world
then child of this poetry
turn against the nature of things

and tell the earth
that you have seen dawn breaking
in the belly of a field.

THE WORLD'S FIRST JUNIOR EXECUTIVE

The world's first junior executive,
Now 87 years old, sits alone in his study
Looking outside, where it seems, buildings
Are collapsing on one another, and he
Still alone these years on,
Draws up the final schedule,
The final business transaction
Between man and God.

This morning the dawn hesitates over Woolworth's
Wondering whether to disturb his phallic dreams
Or let them go on.
Birds of love that once flew in pairs
Now make singular journeys—
He who was not brave about living
Is less brave about dying;
Still, he dies;
And in various offices new executive rise
Not in 'silent tribute'
But to cough and apply
For what his death
Has left open to them.

IN NUMEROUS CITY GARDENS

   . . . And in numerous city gardens
Long legged girls left alone, bow low among the trees,
Heavy with morning sickness
They wish to be eaten by the sun
And to disappear;
And their hair blown blond or black or brown,
Falls across their faces like waterfalls,
And the gardeners know them, those girls
Who break down by the summer houses into tears,
Who left empty now
Wish the boys who have left them to come near.

Lethargically and without much effort
They count on their fingers
The days that are fading,
Lost in their own isolation
They see in each face a continent of sadness
As the secretaries, potent in the sunlight,
And their men, drift past them.
And like children lost in fading grottoes
They see behind transparent cities
Sad empty visions
And detach themselves from living for a while.

★ ★ ★

And now that your heart is able to share in their isolation
What can you possibly see
But an army of days moving towards their end
And those things decay
You thought could not have decayed?

So come close now, and sighing, join in the parade;
Our lives must move gently on the world,
And hurdled together for comfort and for ease
Let us note in separate ways
How we are lost in our isolation
And count on our fingers
The passing of days.

CHIEF INSPECTOR PATTEN AND THE CASE OF THE BROWN THIGH

It's the same old story—
That brown thigh keeps cropping up
In distant conversations.
It wont keep still,
Wriggles through the bedclothes
And out onto the carpet
Where it stands amused,
The blond hairs a little damp;
Reflects nice in that
Red light though.

Mmmm, it crops up in parks
And at parties,
Hiding restless on occasions behind
Neat little jeans.
It must be a delusion, I think,
That brown thigh certainly gets around.
'Yes' you say, somewhat sadly,
'I believe it does . . .'

'Numerous people have come to investigate
It,' he said, 'but I doubt if they've found
Anything new.'
'It must be rather exciting for it' I ventured.

In winter, the brown thigh,
(Slightly paler than last summer)
Sleeps purring. 'Must fetch something
To cover it,' he said, feeling fatherly.
'I doubt if it needs any coverage,' I said,
'It belongs to no body in particular,
It has "Eros" tattooed all over it,
It's investigation's
Been going on for centuries.'

POPPOEM

She's going to allnight parties,
Getting high occasionally,
Then going home to mother
On the first green bus of dawn,
Her blonde hair dishevelled,
Her dress slightly torn.

Busconductor knows her,
Doesn't bother to take her fare,
Seen her on every bus
Knows she makes it anywhere,
Her blonde hair dishevelled,
Her dress slightly torn.

One night at a party
She turned onto cocaine,
Busconductor said
She was never the same again—
She's grown older,
Like us all,
Too many late parties,
Too many problems at dawn . . .

THE FRUITFUL LADY OF DAWN

She walks across the room and opens the skylight
thinking, perhaps a bird will drop in
and teach me how to sing.

She attempts to understand why a sentence made of kisses
is followed by the image
of somebody wandering alone through semi-colons

but cannot fathom out
whose dawn she belongs in,
so among them she is silent

and under the skylight
puts on a red dress calling it a blue one;
she approaches breakfast as she would a lover,

She will not work
but sits smelling flowers
in the pantry.

She is alive,
and one of her body's commonest needs
I have made holy

For she will feed my pink bird,
She will make love in technicolour
She will be the Fruitful Lady of Dawn.

SOMEWHERE BETWEEN HEAVEN AND WOOLWORTH'S

A Song

She keeps kingfishers in their cages
And goldfish in their bowls,
She is lovely and is afraid
Of such things as growing cold.

She's had enough men to please her
Though they were more cruel than kind
And their love an act in isolation,
A form of pantomime.

She says she has forgotten
The feelings that she shared
At various all-night parties
Among the couples on the stairs,

For among the songs and dancing
She was once open wide,
A girl dressed in denim
With boys dressed in lies.

She's eating roses on toast with tulip butter,
Praying for her mirror to stay young;
On its no longer gilted surface
This message she has scrawled:

'O somewhere between Heaven and Woolworth's
I live I love I scold,
I keep kingfishers in their cages
And goldfish in their bowls.'

MAUD, 1965

Maud, where are you Maud?
With your long dresses and peachcream complexion:
In what cage did you hang that black bat night?
What took place in the garden? Maud, it's over,
You can tell us now.

Still lyrical but much used, you wander about the suburbs
Watching the buses go past full of young happy people
Wondering where the garden is, wherever can it be,
And how can it be lost. Maud, it's no use.

Can it be that you got yourself lost
And are living with an out of work musician,
You share a furnished room and have an old wireless
That tells you the latest bad news.
What's happening Maud?

Do you wear a Mary Quant dress?
Where are you? and are you very lost,
Very much alone? Do you have stupendous dreams
And wake with one hand on your breasts
And the other on your cunt?
Do you cry for that garden, lost among pornographic
                                                suggestions
Where the concrete flowers neither open nor close?
Who poured weedkiller over your innocence?

We could not find that garden for you,
Even if we tried.
So, come into the city Maud,
Where flowers are too quickly picked
And the days are murdered like vicious enemies.

Maud, is that you I see
Alone among the office blocks,
Head bowed, young tears singing pop-sorrow
On your cheeks?

SONG OF THE PINK BIRD

Let the pink bird sing; it's at your breast
In a room we're sharing
And your head on my chest confirms
It's glad domination.
Let the world play its games beyond the curtains,
We are certain of only one thing,
Let the pink bird sing.
We have lost interest in wars and political situations,
There are craters in our hearts,
We must not neglect them,
Let the pink bird sing.
Let it sing as long as singing matters,
Look through the curtains
The clouds are blushing,
The moon appologising—
Let the pink bird bring home to us
One reason for living,
Let the pink bird sing.

MAUD—A FRAGMENT (2)

Twenty. It would have been best to have arrived at this age
Grinning and drunk, dressed in poor clothes
With our heads full of dragons.
But we arrive quietly;
Nothing worked out, prepared or accomplished.
Maud, all is not perfect with what our mirror's reflecting.

Perhaps we are past lying.
Able at last to look beneath our dreams,
To see flowers, children—
Those bright things with which we protected ourselves,
Simply excuses.

The city, its half-lives and its relationships,
They no longer reach us.
We sit in our rooms like criminals awaiting the arrival of
                                        their crimes;
I think sometimes
That our hearts have shrunken.

Maud, how thin you have grown!
You are deaf to the messages screamed from transistors,
Blind to the shop windows,
Their fashionable messages meaningless now.

Tonight you stand at this skylight window, wonderous and
                                        silent.
Some bitter, bastard world has stripped you clean of
                                        dreams.

Your breasts hang low,
Now simply a part of you
They do not care for black lace or vanity.

Maud, it is much later now.
Between the concrete banks the rivers of the sky run,
Black estuaries polluted by stars
And daily beneath them
We would ourselves;
Ignorant of any tenderness we hide in each other's lives
A clue to our loneliness.
Boredom shares our beds,
It turns whats living dead in us—
Yet among the drifting populations mock love suits us fine,
We wear our personalities well !
Twenty. Already inside us
Something has fallen asleep

SLEEP NOW

In Memory of Wilfred Owen

Sleep now,
Your blood moving in the quiet wind;
No longer afraid of the rabbits
Hurrying through the tall grass
Or the faces laughing from
The beach and among cold trees.

Sleep now,
Alone in the sleeves of grief,
Listening to clothes falling
And your flesh touching God;
To the chatter and backslapping
Of Christ meeting heroes of war.

Sleep now,
Your words have passed
The lights shining from the East
And the sound of flack
Raping graves and emptying seasons.

You do not hear the dry wind pray
Or the children play a game called soldiers
In the street.

AFTER BREAKFAST

After breakfast,
Which is usually coffee and a view
Of teeming rain and the Cathedral old and grey but
Smelling good with grass and ferns
I go out thinking of all those people who've come into this room
And have slept here
Sad and naked
Alone in pairs
Who came together and
Were they young and white with
Some hint of innocence
Or did they come simply to come, to
Fumble then finally tumble apart;
Or were they older still, past sex,
Lost in mirrors, contemplating their decay and
What did the morning mean to them?

Perhaps once this room was the servant's quarters.
Was she young with freckles, with apple breasts?
Did she ever laugh?
Tease the manservant with her 19th Century charms
And her skirts whirling,
Did she look out through the skylight
And wish she were free, and
What did she have for breakfast?

Waking this morning I think
How good it would be to have someone to share
breakfast with.
Whole familes waking!
A thousand negligées, pyjamas, nightgowns
All wandering warm down to breakfast
How secure! and
Others coming out the far end of dawn

51

Having only drizzle and pain for breakfast
Waking always to be greeted with the poor feast of daylight.

How many half-lives
Sulking behind these windows
From basement to attic
Complaining and asking
Who will inherit me today?
Who will I share breakfast with?
And always the same answer coming back—

The rain will inherit you—lonely breakfaster!

THE BEAST

Something that was not there before
has come through the mirror
into my room.

It is not such a simple creature
as first I thought—
from somewhere it has brought a mischief

that troubles both silence and objects
and now left alone here
I weave intricate reasons for its arrival.

They disintegrate. Today, in January, with
the light frozen on my window, I hear outside
a million panicking birds, and know even out there

comfort is done with; it has shattered
even the stars, this creature
at last come home to me

A GREEN SPORTSCAR

     . . . And later
to come across those couples
in gleaming green sportscars,
rivetted with steel and sprinkled with dawn,
and, still shaking in tarpaulin hoods,
the rain spills onto their faces
and the daylight exposes
its E-type death.

     . . . And later still
to discover inside him, something has been moved.
She is stretched out across him, breasts
pointing towards dawn, who found her last kick
in the sound of the skid on tarmac
of the greensteel coffin in its quiet field

     . . . And lastly,
to understand them; those couples who
having been switched off permanently,
are so very still. You would think them asleep
not dead, if not for their expressions
caught by the dawn and held in the grass,
left as evidence against them.

PARTY PIECE

He said:

'Let's stay here
Now this place has emptied
And make gentle pornography with one another,
While the partygoers go out
And the dawn creeps in,
Like a stranger.

Let us not hesitate
Over what we know
Or over how cold this place has become,
But lets unclip our minds
And let tumble free
The mad, mangled crocodile of love.'

So they did,
There among the woodbines and guinness stains,
And later he caught a bus and she a train
And all there was between them then
was rain.

LOOKING BACK ON IT

At nineteen I was a brave Old Hunchback
Climbing to 'tremendous heights'
Preparing to swing down on my golden rope
And rescue the Accused Innocence.
But on my swooping, downward path one day
Innocence ducked
And I amazed at such an act crashed into
A wall she had been building,
How silly now to think myself able to rescue anything!

IN THE SUBURBS OF THE HEART

Leave what relationships still trouble you
in the cities that bother you; go farther
than the leaves have been, leave

memories, dreams, such things
behind you. Then you'll reach
the suburbs of the heart, that thin place

where lives lay scattered and lovers,
half remembering that they love
touch as if by accident and move away.

In the suburbs of the heart you
will find a soft creature, bring
it here to me; bring it near.

It will almost have grown silent, so lift it
from the branches/of the trees
that could not hear it; bring it near.

Where the roads have thinned out or
the thin roads have ended you
will sense it shivering. If the night

has been cold enough what it is afraid of
will have frozen quite near it. Bring both here.
Do not think you can protect it;

see how in your hands, all creatures tremble.
In the suburbs of the heart what
you love and hate must mingle.

A TALK WITH A WOOD

Moving through you one evening
when you offered shelter to
quiet things soaked in rain

I saw through your thinning branches
the beginnings of suburbs, and
frightened by the rain,

gray hares running upright in
distant fields, and quite alone there
thought of nothing but my footprints

being filled, and love, distilled
of people, drifted free, and then
the woods spoke with me.

IN A NEW KIND OF DAWN

In a new kind of dawn
readjusting your conscience
you wake, and

woken you dream
or so it seems
of forests you've come across

& lives you'd have swum through
had you been strong enough

ON THE DAWN BOAT

on the dawn boat,
coming awake,
the land empty, I thought

about it, about
the many warnings,
the many signs, but

none to lead me away
from here, none
to lead me there.

WHAT YOU SHOULD DO EACH MORNING

At last it cannot matter
what openings are seen through
as long as outside any are

the same still horses, poised
against dawn, so
very white against dawn:

it does not matter
as long as shouting Yes
you rush outside

leaping on any of them then
ride madly away
singing, singing, singing.

TRAVELLING BETWEEEN PLACES

Leaving nothing and nothing ahead;
when you stop for the evening
the sky will be in ruins,

when you hear late birds
with tired throats singing
think how good it is that they,

knowing you were coming,
stayed up late to greet you
who travels between places

when the late afternoon
drifts into the woods, when
nothing matters specially.

GEORGE ALLEN & UNWIN LTD

Head office:
40 Museum Street, London, W.C.1
Telephone: 01-405 8577

Sales, Distribution and Accounts Departments
Park Lane, Hemel Hempstead, Herts.
Telephone: 0442 3244

Argentina: Rodriguez Pena 1653-11B, Buenos Aires
Australia: Cnr. Bridge Road and Jersey Street, Hornsby, N.S.W. 2077
Canada: 2330 Midland Avenue, Agincourt, Ontario
Greece: 7 Stadiou Street, Athens 125
India: 103/5 Fort Street, Bombay 1
285J Bepin Behari Ganguli Street, Calcutta 12
2/18 Mount Road, Madras 2
4/21-22B Asaf Ali Road, New Delhi 1
Japan: 29/13 Hongo 5 Chome, Bunkyo, Tokyo 113
Kenya: P.O. Box 30583, Nairobi
Lebanon: Deeb Building, Jeanne d'Arc Street, Beirut
Mexico: Serapio Randon 125, Mexico 4, D.F.
New Zealand: 46 Lake Road, Northcote, Auckland 9
Nigeria: P.O. Box 62, Ibadan
Pakistan: Karachi Chambers, McLeod Road, Karachi 2
22 Falettis' Hotel, Egerton Road, Lahore
Philippines: 3 Malaming Street, U.P. Village, Quezon City, D-505
Singapore: 248c/1 Orchard Road, Singapore 9
South Africa: P.O. Box 23134, Joubert Park, Johannesburg
West Indies: Rockley New Road, St. Lawrence 4, Barbados